GWEN COSTELLO

Blessed Are You!

A Prayerbook for Catholics

 TWENTY-THIRD PUBLICATIONS

185 WILLOW STREET • PO BOX 180 • MYSTIC, CT 06355
TEL: 1-800-321-0411 • FAX: 1-800-572-0788
E-MAIL: ttpubs@aol.com • www.twentythirdpublications.com

Blessed Are You!

Twenty-Third Publications
A Division of Bayard
185 Willow Street
P.O. Box 180
Mystic, CT 06355
(860) 536-2611
(800) 321-0411
www.twentythirdpublications.com

ISBN:1-58595-260-5
Printed in the U.S.A.

Contents

Introduction

Section 3: Seasonal Prayers

Section 4: Scripture-based Prayers

Section 7: Stations of the Cross

Introduction

Every day is a new opportunity to welcome God into our lives through prayer. God is always present, but for many reasons, we are not always attentive to God's presence. The prayers in this book offer opportunities to spend time with God, particularly in the morning before beginning the tasks of the day and in the evening before going to bed.

Each Morning and Evening Prayer (Sunday through Saturday) contains eight elements:
- Beginning Prayers,
- Readings from Holy Scripture,
- Prayers to Christ,
- Silent Meditation,
- Praying with Mary and the Saints,
- Praying with Creation,
- Intercessory Prayers,
- and Ending Prayers.

You can use all eight elements or pick and choose according to the time available and your own preference. You will notice that occasionally direction is given for prayer motions, bowing your head and raising your hands, for example. These are optional, of course, to be used only if they enhance your time of prayer. Also, should you want to pray these prayers within a group, the ones to be said by a leader are marked with a small cross, and the responses are marked with an "R."

In addition to Morning and Evening Prayers, this book also contains:

- Prayers for Special Occasions and Needs,
- Seasonal Prayers,
- Scripture-based Prayers,
- Traditional Catholic Prayers (some expressed in contemporary language),
- Prayers to and by the Saints,
- and the Stations of the Cross.

The journey into prayer is unique to each person who prays. Yet, the great and mysterious journey of prayer begins the same way for all of us. It happens the moment we lift our minds and hearts to God. May God speak to you through all the rhythms of your days and nights and at every moment in between. And may the prayers herein remind you that you are a pilgrim on the sacred path to God.

Ask and it shall be given to you.
Seek and you shall find;
knock and it shall be opened to you.
For everyone who seeks, finds,
and to those who knock,
the door shall be opened.
Matthew 7:7–8

The Lord is near.
Have no anxiety
but in every prayer and supplication
with thanksgiving
let your petitions be made known to God.
Philippians 4:6

Pray without ceasing,
be attentive to prayer,
and pray in a spirit
of thanksgiving.
Colossians: 4:2

The Spirit helps us in our weakness,
for we do not know
how to pray as we ought,
so that very Spirit intercedes
with sighs too deep for words.
And God, who searches our hearts
knows what the Spirit is asking.
Romans: 8:26–27

SECTION 1

Daily Prayer

Sunday Morning Prayer

Beginning Prayer

Blessed are you, good and gracious God of sunrises and morning light. In you I live and move and have my being; without you I can do nothing. Stir my heart to imitate your compassion, and may I never stray from the path of your light this day. Be with me now as I join my sisters and brothers in homes and churches, in convents and monasteries all over the world in offering you Sunday morning praise.

Bow reverently
R. Holy, holy, holy God, I rejoice in your love for me. May I ever praise you; may I ever love you; may I ever keep you in my heart. Blessed, holy, and glorious are you, God of the morning light.

Holy Scripture

(based on Genesis 6:5–13)

After Noah had completed the ark and his family and all the animals were in it, the rains began to fall, just as the Lord God had said. It rained until all the earth was covered; it rained for forty days and forty nights. As the rain subsided, Noah sent a dove from the ark to search for dry land, and when it returned after the third time, it had an olive branch in its mouth. When Noah and his family disembarked onto dry land, they praised and thanked God for saving them.

Praying to Christ

+ When I doubt your promises to me, Christ Jesus…

R. Remind me that your word is trustworthy.

+ When I am in need of your special protection, Christ Jesus…

R. Remind me that you watch over me always.

+ When I have received great blessings, Christ Jesus…

R. Remind me to offer praise and thanks to God.

Silent Meditation

Bow reverently

Glory be to you, holy, blessed, and glorious Trinity, Father, Son, and Mothering Spirit; I enter now into the silence of your compassionate heart.

Praying with Mary and the Saints

+ Blessed Mother Mary and all you holy angels and saints of God, I join my voice to yours as I prepare for the work of this day.

+ Mother Mary, Queen of heaven and earth

R. Bless those who lead others this day.

+ Mother of Jesus, our example and guide,

R. Bless those who are mothers this day.

+ Mary, Star of the Sea, first and best disciple of Christ,

R. Bless those who preach the gospel this day.

+ Mother Mary, handmaid of the Lord,

R. Bless all who say yes to God this day.

Blessed Mary and all you holy angels and saints of God, surround me and challenge me this day to do all that God asks of me.

Praying with Creation

+ Sun and moon, stars and planets, galaxies and endless space…

R. Give praise to God, our holy Creator God.

+ Mountains and valleys, rivers and streams, forests and plains…

R. Give praise to Christ, our holy Savior God.

+ Birds and beasts, fishes and all water creatures, wild animals and household pets…

R. Give praise to the Spirit, our holy Companion God.

All creatures great and small praise you, O God. May I, too, praise you by striving to be what you have created me to be.

Intercessions

Extend your hands, palms upward

As I begin this first day of the week, Christ Jesus, I ask your blessing on all your people.

R. Fill them with your faith, hope, and love.

+ Be with those who travel to work this day and bless their efforts.

R. Fill them with your faith, hope, and love.

+ Be with all the children of the world this day, especially those who are hungry and afraid.

R. Fill them with your faith, hope, and love.

+ Be mindful of the poor, the hungry, the downtrodden this day.

R. Fill them with your faith, hope, and love.

+Have mercy on those who are suffering: the sick, the dying, the despairing, the depressed, and carry to yourself

all who have recently died, especially_____.
R. Fill them with your faith, hope, and love.
I pray now in the silence of my heart for these
personal intentions…

Ending Prayer

Bow reverently

Holy Savior Jesus, I go forth now to practice your love and to share it. Come with me, please, that I may not grow weary. May I do nothing on this Sunday that I will regret, or harm others in any way. Come with me, Christ Jesus, as I begin the sacred journey of this first day of the week. Amen.

Sunday Evening Prayer

Beginning Prayer

Blessed are you, good and gracious God of sunsets and evening stars. I end this first day of the week hoping that I have given you praise and thanksgiving with my whole heart, mind, and soul. You have been with me in all that I have done this day and you will be with me as I sleep. Give me holy rest this night and deep peace. Forgive me for any wrong I have done to you, O God, and to others. Absolve me from the sins I have committed and any good deeds I have omitted.

Bow reverently

R. Holy, holy, holy God, you love me and you forgive me. Blessed, holy, and glorious are you, my God, compassionate and loving, this night and forever.

Holy Scripture

(based on Matthew 5:13–16)

Jesus said to his followers, "You are the salt of the earth, but if salt loses its taste, it is good for nothing and has to be thrown out. You are the light of the world. A city built on a hilltop cannot be hidden. No one lights a lamp and then covers it up. Rather they put it in a place where it shines on everyone in the house. In the same way, your light must shine that you may be an example to others, so that when people see your good works, they may give praise to their Father in heaven.

Praying to Christ

+ I want to be the salt of the earth, Christ Jesus…

R. Teach me how to flavor my world with truth and goodness.

+ I want to be a light for the world, Christ Jesus…

R. Please let your light shine through me.

+ I want to give witness to your light and power, Christ Jesus…

R. Strengthen me to follow you today and always.

Silent Meditation

Bow Reverently

Glory be to you, holy, blessed, and glorious Trinity, Father, Son, and Mothering Spirit. I enter now into the silence of your compassionate heart.

Praying with Mary and the Saints

+ Blessed Mother Mary and all you holy angels and saints of God, I join my voice to yours this night as I prepare for my rest…

+ Saint Nicodemus, disciple and friend of Jesus,

R. Bless those who are seeking God's truth this day.

+ Saint Peter Claver, comforter of the slaves,

R. Bless those who are working for freedom this day.

+ Saint Lazarus, raised from the dead by Jesus,

R. Bless those who are struggling to survive this day.

+ Saint Kevin, faithful follower of Jesus,

R. Bless all who are living the gospel this day.

Blessed Mary and all you holy angels and saints of God, surround me, bless me, and keep me company this night that I might rest in God.

Praying with Creation

> + Day and night, sun and clouds, cold and heat, wind and rain, ice and snow…
>
> R. Give praise to God, our holy Creator God.
>
> + Winter and spring, summer and fall, and all of life's seasons…
>
> R. Give praise to Christ, our holy Savior God.
>
> + Flowers and trees, meadows and forests, fields and farms, rain forests and deserts…
>
> R. Give praise to the Spirit, our holy Companion God.
>
> All creatures great and small give you praise, O God. May I, too, praise you by being what you have called me to be.

Intercessions

Extend your hands, palms upward

> As I end this day, Christ Jesus, I ask your blessing on all your people.
>
> R. Fill them with your grace and goodness.
>
> + Watch over my family members, my friends, my coworkers, and all who have asked for my prayers.
>
> R. Fill them with your grace and goodness.
>
> + Watch over all the world's children this night and may your angels guide their dreams and keep them from fear.
>
> R. Fill them with your grace and goodness.
>
> + Be mindful of all laborers and bless their rest that they may prosper tomorrow with your grace.
>
> R. Fill them with your grace and goodness.
>
> + Have mercy on those who are suffering: the sick, the dying, the despairing, the depressed, and carry to yourself all those who have recently died, especially_____.

R. Fill them with your grace and goodness.

I pray now in the silence of my heart for these personal intentions...

Ending Prayer

Bow reverently

Holy Savior Jesus, stay with me, for night has come and I want to rest in you. Stay with me, for I need your forgiveness before I sleep. Stay with me, Christ Jesus, as I seek the sacred peace of those who place their faith in you. Amen.

Monday Morning Prayer

Beginning Prayer

Blessed are you, good and gracious God of sunrises and morning light. In you I live and move and have my being; without you I can do nothing. Stir my heart to imitate your compassion, and may I never stray from the path of your light this day. Be with me now as I join my sisters and brothers in homes and churches, in convents and monasteries all over the world in offering you Monday morning praise.

Bow reverently
R. Holy, holy, holy God, I rejoice in your love for me. May I ever praise you; may I ever serve you; may you ever dwell within my heart. Blessed, holy, and glorious are you, God of the morning light.

Holy Scripture
(based on Genesis 15:1–6)

Abraham and Sarah could have no children and Abraham complained to God. "What do you intend for me; I am old and childless?" But God said to Abraham, "Have faith in me. Look up to heaven and count the stars if you can. Just so will your descendants be." And Abraham put his faith in God.

Praying to Christ

+ When I have lost faith that you are guiding me,
Christ Jesus…

R. Remind me that you watch over me always.

+ When I forget that you can do wonders for me,
Christ Jesus…

R. Remind me that your love is all powerful.

+ When I forget to look up at the stars, Christ Jesus…

R. Remind me that God gives me countless blessings.

Silent Meditation

Bow reverently

Glory be to you, holy, blessed, and glorious Trinity, Father, Son, and Mothering Spirit. I enter now into the silence of your compassionate heart.

Praying with Mary and the Saints

+ Blessed Mother Mary and all you holy angels and saints of God, I join my voice to yours as I prepare for the work of this day.

+ Saint Ann, Mother of Mary, wife of Joachim,

R. Bless those who work in the home this day.

+ Saint Matthew, tax collector and disciple,

R. Bless those who work in the marketplace this day.

+ Saint Benedict, monk and contemplative,

R. Bless those who pray for the world this day.

+ Saint Monica, mother of Augustine,

R. Bless the work of all parents this day.

Blessed Mary and all you holy angels and saints of God, surround me and challenge me this day to do all that God asks of me.

Praying with Creation

+ Sun and moon, stars and planets, galaxies and endless space…

R. Give praise to God, our holy Creator God.

+ Mountains and valleys, rivers and streams, forests and plains…

R. Give praise to Christ, our holy Savior God.

+ Birds and beasts, fishes and all water creatures, wild animals and household pets…

R. Give praise to the Spirit, our holy Companion God.

All creatures great and small praise you, O God. May I, too, praise you by striving to be what you have created me to be.

Intercessions

Extend your hands, palms upward

As I begin this new day of life, Christ Jesus, I ask your blessing on all your people.

R. Fill them with your compassion and love.

+ Be with those who travel to work and bless their efforts this day and the efforts of their coworkers.

R. Fill them with your compassion and love.

+ Watch over the world's children this day, especially those who are lonely and afraid.

R. Fill them with your compassion and love.

+ Be mindful of all who labor in factories and fields this day and bless the work of their hands.

R. Fill them with your compassion and love.

+ Have mercy on those who are suffering: the sick, the dying, the despairing, the depressed, and carry to yourself all who have recently died, especially_____.

R. Fill them with your compassion and love.

I pray now in the silence of my heart for these personal intentions…

Ending Prayer

Bow reverently

Holy Savior Jesus, I go forth now to practice your love and to share it. Come with me, please, that I may not grow weary. May I do nothing on this Monday that I will regret, or harm others in any way. Come with me, Christ Jesus, as I begin the sacred journey of this day. Amen.

Monday Evening Prayer

Beginning Prayer

Blessed are you God of sunsets and evening stars. I end
this first day of the week hoping that I have given you
praise and thanksgiving with my whole heart, mind, and
soul. You have been with me in all that I have done this
day and you will be with me as I sleep. Give me holy rest
this night and deep peace. Forgive me for any wrong I
have done to you, O God, and to others. Absolve me from
the sins I have committed and any good deeds I have
omitted.

Bow reverently
R. Holy, holy, holy God, you love me and you forgive me.
Blessed, holy, and glorious are you, my God, compassion-
ate and loving, this night and forever.

Holy Scripture
(based on Matthew 15:32–38)
And the Lord Jesus, when he saw all the people growing
weary, said to his followers, "We have to feed these people
something; otherwise they won't make it home. See how
tired they are, and yet they stay on to listen to me." But
they had very little food, only seven loaves and a few small
fishes. Blessing what they had, Jesus told his followers to
distribute it, and then all four thousand people had plenty
to eat. After all had eaten, there were seven baskets left
over.

Praying to Christ

+ I have come to listen to you, Christ Jesus…

R. Feed me with the bread of life.

+ I have come to find the truth, Christ Jesus…

R. Feed me with the bread of truth.

+ I have come to you hungry, Christ Jesus…

R. Feed me with the loaves and fishes of your grace.

Silent Meditation

Bow reverently

Glory be to you, holy, blessed, and glorious Trinity, Father, Son, and Mothering Spirit. I enter now into the silence of your compassionate heart.

Praying with Mary and the Saints

+ Blessed Mother Mary and all you holy angels and saints of God, I join my voice to yours this night as I prepare for my rest…

+ Saint Joseph, carpenter and father,

R. Bless those who have worked with their hands this day.

+ Saint Thérèse, religious and contemplative,

R. Bless those who have prayed for the world this day.

+ Saint Patrick, priest and missionary,

R. Bless those who have proclaimed the gospel this day.

+ Saint Dismas, the repentant good thief,

R. Bless those who have been humble and honest this day. Blessed Mary and all you holy angels and saints of God, surround me, bless me, and keep me company this night that I might rest in God.

Praying with Creation

+ Day and night, sun and clouds, cold and heat, wind and rain, ice and snow…

R. Give praise to God, our holy Creator God.

+ Winter and spring, summer and fall, and all of life's seasons…

R. Give praise to Christ, our holy Savior God.

+ Flowers and trees, meadows and forests, fields and farms, rain forests and deserts…

R. Give praise to the Spirit, our holy Companion God.

All creatures great and small praise you, O God. May I, too, praise you by being what you have called me to be.

Intercessions

Extend your hands, palms upward

As I end this day, Christ Jesus, I ask your blessing on all your people.

R. Fill them with your peace and goodness.

+ Watch over my family members, my friends, my coworkers, and all who have asked for my prayers.

R. Fill them with your peace and goodness.

+ Watch over children everywhere this night, and may your angels guide their dreams and keep them from fear.

R. Fill them with your peace and goodness.

+ Be mindful of all who have labored and bless their rest that they may be restored.

R. Fill them with your peace and goodness.

+ Have mercy on those who are suffering: the sick, the dying, the despairing, the depressed, and carry to yourself all those who have recently died, especially_____.

R. Fill them with your peace and goodness.

I pray now in the silence of my heart for these personal intentions…

Ending Prayer

Bow reverently

Holy Savior Jesus, stay with me, for night has come and I want to rest in you. Stay with me, for I need your forgiveness before I sleep. Stay with me, Christ Jesus, as I seek the sacred peace of those who place their faith in you. Amen.

Tuesday Morning Prayer

Beginning Prayer

Blessed are you, good and gracious God of sunrises and morning light. In you I live and move and have my being; without you I can do nothing. Stir my heart to imitate your compassion, and may I never stray from the path of your light this day. Be with me now as I join my sisters and brothers in homes and churches, in convents and monasteries all over the world in offering you Tuesday morning praise.

Bow reverently
R. Holy, holy, holy God, I rejoice in your love for me. May I ever praise you; may I ever serve you; may you ever dwell within my heart. Blessed, holy, and glorious are you, God of the morning light.

Holy Scripture
(based on Isaiah 58:9–11)

When you cry out, God will answer. When you call, God will say: "Here I am." When you put away your anger, when you give food to the hungry and lighten the burdens of others, your light will rise in the darkness and your gloom will banish in the midday sun. You will be like a well-watered garden that never runs dry.

Praying to Christ

+ When I forget that I am called to be light for the afflicted, Christ Jesus…

R. Remind me that you will show me the way.

+ When I have done deeds of darkness, Christ Jesus…

R. Remind me that you always forgive me.

+ When I forget that you walk with me always, Christ Jesus…

R. Remind me that you are light and goodness.

Silent Meditation

Bow reverently

Glory be to you, holy, blessed, and glorious Trinity, Father, Son, and Mothering Spirit. I enter now into the silence of your compassionate heart.

Praying with Mary and the Saints

+ Blessed Mother Mary and all you holy angels and saints of God, I join my voice to yours as I prepare for the work of this day.

+ Saint Thomas More, husband, father, and lawyer,

R. Bless all who work for justice this day.

+ Saint Peter, fisherman and apostle,

R. Bless those who work on the water this day.

+ Saint John Bosco, teacher and model,

R. Bless those who teach others this day.

+ Saint Martha, sister of Mary and Lazarus,

R. Bless those who prepare meals this day.

Blessed Mary and all you holy angels and saints of God, surround me and challenge me this day to do the will of our holy, blessed, and glorious God.

Praying with Creation

+ Sun and moon, stars and planets, galaxies and endless space…

R. Give praise to God, our holy Creator God.

+ Mountains and valleys, rivers and streams, forests and plains…

R. Give praise to Christ, our holy Savior God.

+ Birds and beasts, fishes and all water creatures, wild animals and household pets…

R. Give praise to the Spirit, our Holy Companion God.

All creatures great and small praise you, O God. May I, too, praise you by striving to be what you have created me to be.

Intercessions

Extend your hands, palms upward

+ As I begin this new day of life, Lord Jesus, I ask your blessing on all your people.

R. Fill them with your love and joy.

+ Be with those who travel to work this day and bless their efforts at the workplace.

R. Fill them with your love and joy.

+ Watch over all children throughout the world and keep them safe from fear and suffering.

R. Fill them with your love and joy.

+ Be mindful of the poor and the hungry this day.

R. Fill them with your love and joy.

+ Have mercy on those who are suffering: the sick, the dying, the despairing, the depressed, and carry to yourself all those who have recently died, especially_____.

R. Fill them with your love and joy.

I pray now in the silence of my heart for these
personal intentions…

Ending Prayer

Bow reverently

Holy Savior Jesus, I go forth now to practice your love
and to share it. Come with me, please, that I may
not grow weary. May I do nothing on this Tuesday that I
will regret, or harm others in any way. Come with me,
Christ Jesus, as I begin the sacred journey of this day.
Amen.

Tuesday Evening Prayer

Beginning Prayer

Blessed are you, God of sunsets and evening stars. I end this day hoping that I have given you praise and thanksgiving with my whole heart, mind and soul. You have been with me in all that I have done this day and you will be with me as I sleep. Give me holy rest this night and deep peace. Forgive me for any wrong I have done to you, O God, and to others. Absolve me from the sins I have committed and any good deeds I have omitted.

Bow reverently
R. Holy, holy, holy God, you love me and you forgive me. Blessed, holy, and glorious are you, my God, compassionate and loving, this night and forever.

Holy Scripture
(based on Mark 8:22–26)

The people brought a blind man to Jesus and Jesus led him to the edge of town, where he used his own saliva and rubbed it on the man's eyes. "Can you see?" he asked the blind man. "Yes, I see people, but they look like walking trees." And so Jesus put more saliva on the man's eyes, and then the man saw everything clearly.

Praying to Christ

+ I have come to be healed by you, Christ Jesus…

R. Cleanse me of all sin and weakness.

+ I want to see you more clearly, Christ Jesus…

R. Open my eyes and my heart to receive you.

+ I have come to you spiritually blind, Christ Jesus…

R. Send me your Spirit of light and grace.

Silent Meditation

Bow reverently

Glory be to you, holy, blessed, and glorious Trinity, Father, Son, and Mothering Spirit. I enter now into the silence of your compassionate heart.

Praying with Mary and the Saints

+ Blessed Mother Mary and all you holy angels and saints of God, I join my voice to yours this night as I prepare for my rest…

+ Saint Vincent Pallotti, priest and prophet,

R. Bless those who have given witness to God this day.

+ Saint Maria Goretti, child and martyr,

R. Bless those who have chosen to do what is right this day.

+ Saint Brendan, priest and missionary,

R. Bless those who have been traveling this day.

+ Saint Sebastian, soldier and martyr,

R. Bless those who were called to battle this day.

Blessed Mary and all you holy angels and saints of God, surround me, bless me, and keep me company this night that I might rest in God.

Praying with Creation

+ Day and night, sun and clouds, cold and heat, wind and rain, ice and snow…

R. Give praise to God, our holy Creator God.

+ Winter and spring, summer and fall, and all of life's seasons…

R. Give praise to Christ, our holy Savior God.

+ Flowers and trees, meadows and forests, fields and farms, rain forests and deserts…

R. Give praise to the Spirit, our holy Companion God.

All creatures great and small praise you, O God. May I, too, praise you by becoming what you have created me to be.

Intercessions

Extend your hands, palms upward

As I end this day, Lord Jesus, I ask your blessing on all your people.

R. Fill them with your patience and peace.

+ Watch over our family members, our friends, our coworkers, and all who have asked for our prayers.

R. Fill them with your patience and peace.

+ Watch over all children this night and may your angels guide their dreams and keep them from fear.

R. Fill them with your patience and peace.

+ Be mindful of all who have labored this day and bless their rest that they may be renewed.

R. Fill them with your patience and peace.

+ Have mercy on those who are suffering: the sick, the dying, the despairing, the depressed, and carry to yourself all those who have recently died, especially_____.

R. Fill them with your patience and peace.

I pray now in the silence of my heart for these personal intentions...

Ending Prayer

Bow reverently

Holy Savior Jesus, stay with me, for night has come and I want to rest in you. Stay with me, for I need your forgiveness before I sleep. Stay with me, Christ Jesus, as I seek the sacred peace of those who trust in you. Amen.

Wednesday Morning Prayer

Beginning Prayer

Blessed are you, good and gracious God of sunrises and morning light. In you I live and move and have my being; without you I can do nothing. Stir my heart to imitate your compassion, and may I never stray from the path of your light this day. Be with me now as I join my sisters and brothers in homes and churches, in convents and monasteries all over the world in offering you Wednesday morning praise.

Bow reverently
R. Holy, holy, holy God, I rejoice in your love for me. May I ever praise you; may I ever serve you; may I ever keep you in my heart. Blessed, holy, and glorious are you, God of the morning light.

Holy Scripture

(based on Exodus 32:1–10)

While Moses was on the mountain communing with God, the people used his absence to create a "God" they could see and touch, a God they could control and carry around. They made themselves a golden calf, and they worshiped this calf, forgetting that Moses had gone up the mountain to commune with the living God, the one true God, to receive the law of life.

Praying to Christ

> \+ When I crave a God I can manipulate, Christ Jesus…
>
> R. Remind me that God is mystery and love.
>
> \+ When I bow down to created things, Christ Jesus…
>
> R. Remind me that God alone is of infinite worth.
>
> \+ When I forget God's true law of life, Christ Jesus…
>
> R. Remind me that without God I can do nothing.

Silent Meditation

> *Bow reverently*
>
> Glory be to you, holy, blessed, and glorious Trinity, Father, Son, and Mothering Spirit. I enter now into the silence of your compassionate heart.

Praying with Mary and the Saints

> \+ Blessed Mother Mary and all you holy angels and saints of God, I join my voice to yours as I prepare for the work of this day.
>
> \+ Saint Mary Magdalene, friend and follower of Jesus,
>
> R. Bless those who listen to God's Word this day.
>
> \+ Saint John the evangelist, beloved disciple of Jesus,
>
> R. Bless those who act upon God's Word this day.
>
> \+ Saint Francis of Assisi, lover of all created things,
>
> R. Bless those who cherish the earth this day.
>
> \+ Saint Augustine, teacher and bishop,
>
> R. Bless those who proclaim the gospel this day.
>
> Blessed Mary and all you holy angels and saints, surround me and challenge me this day to do the will of our holy, blessed, and glorious God.

Praying with Creation

+ Sun and moon, stars and planets, galaxies and endless space…

R. Give praise to God, our holy Creator God.

+ Mountains and valleys, rivers and streams, forests and plains…

R. Give praise to Christ, our holy Savior God.

+ Birds and beasts, fishes and all water creatures, wild animals and household pets…

R. Give praise to the Spirit, our holy Companion God.

All creatures great and small praise you, O God. May I, too, praise you by striving to be what you have called me to be.

Intercessions

Extend your hands, palms upward

As I begin this new day of life, Lord Jesus, I ask your blessing on all your people.

R. Fill them with your courage and wisdom.

+ Bless those who travel to work this day and bless their efforts in the workplace.

R. Fill them with your courage and wisdom.

+ Watch over children everywhere this day, especially those who are lonely and afraid.

R. Fill them with your courage and wisdom.

+ Be mindful of the poor and the hungry this day.

R. Fill them with your courage and wisdom.

+ Have mercy on those who are suffering: the sick, the dying, the despairing, the depressed, and carry to yourself all those who have recently died, especially_____.

R. Fill them with your courage and wisdom.

I pray now in the silence of my heart for these personal intentions…

Ending Prayer

Bow reverently

Holy Savior Jesus, I go forth now to practice your love and to share it. Come with me, please, that I may not grow weary. May I do nothing on this Wednesday that I will regret, or harm others in any way. Come with me, Christ Jesus, as I begin the sacred journey of this day. Amen.

Wednesday Evening Prayer

Beginning Prayer

Blessed are you, God of sunsets and evening stars. I end this day hoping that I have given you praise and thanksgiving with my whole heart, mind, and soul. You have been with me in all that I have done this day and you will be with me as I sleep. Give me holy rest this night and deep peace. Forgive me for any wrong I have done to you, O God, and to others. Absolve me from the sins I have committed and any good deeds I have omitted.

Bow reverently

R. Holy, holy, holy God, you love me and you forgive me. Blessed, holy, and glorious are you God, compassionate and loving, this night and forever.

Holy Scripture

(based on Matthew 7:7–11)

Jesus said to his followers, "Ask and you will receive, seek and you will find, knock and it will be opened to you." Then he admonished them for their lack of faith in their heavenly father who gives good things to those who ask, those who seek, those who knock.

Praying to Christ

+ I want to believe that God listens to my prayers, Christ Jesus…

R. Help me to pray even when it's difficult.

+ I want to knock and be in God's presence, Christ Jesus…

R. Strengthen me to keep asking and knocking.

+ I want to believe in the power of God's love, Christ Jesus…

R. May all I do today give witness to God's gifts in my life.

Silent Meditation

Bow reverently

Glory be to you, holy, blessed, and glorious Trinity, Father, Son, and Mothering Spirit. I enter now into the silence of your compassionate heart.

Praying with Mary and the Saints

+ Blessed Mother Mary and all you holy angels and saints of God, I join my voice to yours this night as I prepare for my rest…

+ Saint Cecilia, patroness of musicians,

R. Bless those who have made music this day.

+ Saint Richard, faithful and courageous king,

R. Bless those who have been good leaders this day.

+ Saint Elizabeth Ann Seton, teacher and mother,

R. Bless all who have taught with wisdom this day.

+ Saint Martin de Porres, caretaker of the poor,

R. Bless those who have worked with the poor this day.

Blessed Mary and all you holy angels and saints of God,

surround me, bless me, and keep me company this night that I might rest in God.

Praying with Creation

+ Day and night, sun and clouds, cold and heat, wind and rain, ice and snow…

R. Give praise to God, our holy Creator God.

+ Winter and spring, summer and fall, and all of life's seasons…

R. Give praise to Christ, our holy Savior God.

+ Flowers and trees, meadows and forests, fields and farms, rain forests and deserts…

R. Give praise to the Spirit, our holy Companion God.

All creatures great and small give you praise, O God. May I, too, praise you by striving to be what you have called me to be.

Intercessions

Extend your hands, palms upward

As I end this day, Christ Jesus, I ask your blessing upon all your people.

R. Fill them with your courage and joy.

+ Watch over my family members, my friends, my coworkers, and all who have asked for my prayers.

R. Fill them with your courage and joy.

+ Watch over all children this night and may your angels guide their dreams and keep them from fear.

R. Fill them with your courage and joy.

+ Be mindful of those who have labored this day and bless their rest that they may be renewed.

R. Fill them with your courage and joy.

+ Have mercy on those who are suffering: the sick, the dying, the despairing, the depressed, and carry to yourself all those who have recently died, especially_____.

R. Fill them with your courage and joy.

I pray now in the silence of my heart for these personal intentions…

Ending Prayer

Bow reverently

Holy Savior Jesus, stay with me, for night has come and I want to rest in you. Stay with me, for I need your forgiveness before I sleep. Stay with me, Christ Jesus, as I seek the sacred peace of those who trust in you. Amen.

Thursday Morning Prayer

Beginning Prayer

Blessed are you, good and gracious God of sunrises and morning light. In you I live and move and have my being; without you I can do nothing. Stir my heart to imitate your compassion, and may I never stray from the path of your light this day. Be with me now as I join my sisters and brothers in homes and churches, in convents and monasteries all over the world in offering you Thursday morning praise.

Bow reverently
R. Holy, holy, holy God, I rejoice in your love for me. May I ever praise you; may I ever serve you; may you ever dwell within my heart. Blessed, holy, and glorious are you, God of the morning light.

Holy Scripture

(based on Job: 38–42)

The Lord God spoke to Job out of the whirlwind… "Where were you when I laid the foundation of the earth…when the morning stars sang together and all the heavenly beings shouted for joy? Have you commanded morning to come and the dawn to know its place? Have you entered into the springs of the sea or walked in the recesses of the deep?" And Job, thus humbled, replied, "I know now that you can do all things and that no purpose of yours can be thwarted."

Praying to Christ

+ When I am tempted to doubt God's wisdom, Christ
Jesus…

R. Remind me that God is all-knowing, all-loving.

+ When I forget to give thanks for all that God has made,
Christ Jesus…

R. Remind me to offer my thanks and praise.

+ When I forget to cherish the earth and all that God has
created, Christ Jesus…

R. Remind me that God is the creator of all.

Silent Meditation

Bow reverently

Glory be to you, holy, blessed, and glorious Trinity, Father,
Son, and Mothering Spirit. I enter now into the silence of
your compassionate heart.

Praying with Mary and the Saints

+ Blessed Mother Mary and all you holy angels and saints
of God, I join my voice to yours as I prepare for the work
of this day.

+ Saint Julian of Norwich, mystic and counselor,

R. Bless those who search for God this day.

+ Saint Bernadette, beloved child of Mary,

R. Bless those who see great wonders this day.

+ Saint Gerard, bishop and martyr,

R. Bless those who guide the church this day.

+ Saint Casimir, peacemaker for God,

R. Bless those who work for peace this day.

Blessed Mary and all you holy angels and saints, surround

me and challenge me this day to do the will of our holy, blessed, and glorious God.

Praying with Creation

> + Sun and moon, stars and planets, galaxies and endless space…
>
> R. Give praise to God, our holy Creator God.
>
> + Mountains and valleys, rivers and streams, forests and plains…
>
> R. Give praise to Christ, our holy Savior God.
>
> + Birds and beasts, fishes and all water creatures, wild animals and household pets…
>
> R. Give praise to the Spirit, our holy Companion God.
>
> All creatures great and small give you praise, O God. May I, too, praise you by striving to be what you have created me to be.

Intercessions

> *Extend your hands, palms upward*
>
> As I begin this new day of life, Lord Jesus, I ask your blessing on all your people.
>
> R. Fill them with your courage and wisdom.
>
> + Be with those who travel to work and bless their efforts in the workplace this day.
>
> R. Fill them with your courage and wisdom.
>
> + Watch over children everywhere this day, especially those who are homeless and afraid.
>
> R. Fill them with your courage and wisdom.
>
> + Be mindful of the poor and the hungry this day.
>
> R. Fill them with your courage and wisdom.

+ Have mercy on those who are suffering: the sick, the dying, the despairing, the depressed, and carry to yourself all those who have recently died, especially_____.
R. Fill them with your courage and wisdom.
I pray now in the silence of my heart for these personal intentions...

Ending Prayer
Bow reverently

Holy Savior Jesus, I go forth now to practice your love and to share it. Come with me, please, that I may not grow weary. May I do nothing on this Thursday that I will regret, or harm others in any way. Come with me, Christ Jesus, as I begin the sacred journey of this day. Amen.

Thursday Evening Prayer

Beginning Prayer

Blessed are you, God of sunsets and evening stars. I end this day hoping that I have given you praise and thanksgiving with my whole heart, mind, and soul. You have been with me in all that I have done this day, and you will be with me as I sleep. Give me holy rest this night and deep peace. Forgive me for any wrong I have done to you, O God, and to others. Pardon me if I have not done my best in the workplace and at home. Absolve me from the sins I have committed and any good deeds I have omitted.

Bow reverently
R. Holy, holy, holy God, you love me and you forgive me. Blessed, holy, and glorious are you, my God, compassionate and loving, this night and forever.

Holy Scripture
(based on John 10:1–5)

Jesus said to his followers, "Anyone who doesn't use the gate to enter a pasture is a thief. The one who enters through the gate is the shepherd of the flock. The sheep hear his voice, and one by one the shepherd calls the sheep and leads them out. When he has brought them out, he goes ahead of them and the sheep follow because they know who he is."

Praying to Christ

+ I want you to be my shepherd, Christ Jesus…

R. Guide me and protect me from all harm.

+ I want to be a shepherd for others, Christ Jesus…

R. Give me the courage to imitate your love.

+ I want to rely on you for everything, Christ Jesus…

R. Help me to rest in your compassionate care.

Silent Meditation

Bow reverently

Glory be to you, holy, blessed, and glorious Trinity, Father, Son, and Mothering Spirit. I enter now into the silence of your compassionate heart.

Praying with Mary and the Saints

+ Blessed Mother Mary and all you holy angels and saints of God, I join my voice to yours this night as I prepare for my rest…

+ Saint Gwendolen, widow and martyr,

R. Bless those who have been courageous this day.

+ Saint Edith Stein, convert and contemplative

R. Bless those who have lived their faith this day.

+ Saint Brigid, abbess and worker of wonders,

R. Bless all who did great things for others this day.

+ Saint Anthony, monk and hermit,

R. Bless all who took time to pray this day.

Blessed Mary and all you holy angels and saints of God, surround me, bless me, and keep me company this night that I might rest in God's loving embrace.

Praying with Creation

+ Day and night, sun and clouds, cold and heat, wind and rain, ice and snow...

R. Give praise to God, our holy Creator God.

+ Winter and spring, summer and fall, and all of life's seasons...

R. Give praise to Christ, our holy Savior God.

+ Flowers and trees, meadows and forests, fields and farms, rain forests and deserts...

R. Give praise to the Spirit, our holy Companion God.

All creatures great and small give you praise, O God. May I, too, praise you by striving to be what you have called me to be.

Intercessions

Extend your hands, palms upward

As I end this day, Christ Jesus, I ask your blessing upon all your people.

R. Fill them with your grace and goodness.

+ Watch over my family members, my friends, my coworkers, and all who have asked for my prayers.

R. Fill them with your grace and goodness.

+ Watch over all children this night and may your angels guide their dreams and keep them from fear.

R. Fill them with your grace and goodness.

+ Be mindful of laborers this day and bless their rest that they may be renewed.

R. Fill them with your grace and goodness.

+ Have mercy on those who are suffering: the sick, the dying, the despairing, the depressed, and carry to yourself all those who have recently died, especially_____.

R. Fill them with your grace and goodness.

I pray now in the silence of my heart for these personal intentions…

Ending Prayer

Bow reverently

Holy Savior Jesus, stay with me, for night has come and I want to rest in you. Stay with me, for I need your forgiveness before I sleep. Stay with me, Christ Jesus, as I seek the sacred peace of those who place their trust in you. Amen.

Friday Morning Prayer

Beginning Prayer

Blessed are you, good and gracious God of sunrises and morning light. In you I live and move and have my being; without you I can do nothing. Stir my heart to imitate your compassion, and may I never stray from the path of your light this day. Be with me now as I join my sisters and brothers in homes and churches, in convents and monasteries all over the world in offering you Friday morning praise.

Bow reverently

R. Holy, holy, holy God, I rejoice in your love for me. May I ever praise you; may I ever serve you; may you ever dwell within my heart. Blessed, holy, and glorious are you, God of the morning light.

Holy Scripture

(based on Jonah 1:1–4; 3:1–10)

The Lord God directed Jonah to go to the Ninevites and call them to repentance. But Jonah rebelled against this command of the Lord. To escape God's call, Jonah got on a boat and sailed away. But when a great storm arose, the sailors blamed Jonah and they pitched him overboard where he might have died had he not fallen into the mouth of a great whale. For three days and three nights he was within the whale and on the third day when the whale spat him out, Jonah again heard God's call. This time he did as God commanded, and the Ninevites turned their hearts toward God.

Praying to Christ

+ When I try to escape my call to follow you, Christ Jesus…

R. Remind me that your call brings light and joy.

+ When I think that you are too forgiving of sinners, Christ Jesus…

R. Remind me that you love sinners and saints alike.

+ When I am too selfish to share your Word, Christ Jesus…

R. Remind me that your Word is for everyone.

Silent Meditation

Bow reverently

Glory be to you, holy, blessed, and glorious Trinity, Father, Son, and Mothering Spirit. I enter now into the silence of your compassionate heart.

Praying with Mary and the Saints

+ Blessed Mother Mary and all you holy angels and saints of God, I join my voice to yours as I prepare for the work of this day.

+ Saint Andrew, apostle and fisherman,

R. Bless those who fish for a living this day.

+ Saint Joachim, father of our Blessed Mother,

R. Bless all who are fathers this day.

+ Saint Francis Xavier, priest and missionary,

R. Bless all who preach in mission lands this day.

+ Saint Ida, holy woman and mystic,

R. Bless all who place their hope in God this day.

Blessed Mary and all you holy angels and saints of God, surround me and challenge me this day to do all that God asks of me with a loving and willing heart.

Praying with Creation

> + Sun and moon, stars and planets, galaxies and endless space…
>
> R. Give praise to God, our holy Creator God.
>
> + Mountains and valleys, rivers and streams, forests and plains…
>
> R. Give praise to Christ, our holy Savior God.
>
> + Birds and beasts, fishes and all water creatures, wild animals and household pets…
>
> R. Give praise to the Spirit, our holy Companion God.
>
> All creatures great and small give you praise, O God. May I, too, praise you by striving to be all that you have called me to be.

Intercessions

> *Extend your hands, palms upward*
>
> As I begin this new day of life, Christ Jesus, I ask your blessing on all your people.
>
> R. Fill them with your understanding and joy.
>
> + Be with those who travel to work this day and bless their efforts in the workplace.
>
> R. Fill them with your understanding and joy.
>
> + Watch over all children throughout the world this day and keep them safe and out of harm's way.
>
> R. Fill them with your understanding and joy.
>
> + Be mindful of the poor and the hungry this day.
>
> R. Fill them with your understanding and joy.
>
> + Have mercy on those who are suffering: the sick, the dying, the despairing, the depressed, and carry to yourself all who have recently died, especially_____.

R. Fill them with your understanding and joy.

I pray now in the silence of my heart for these personal intentions…

Ending Prayer

Bow reverently

Holy Savior Jesus, I go forth now to practice your love and to share it. Come with me, please, that I may not grow weary. May I do nothing on this Friday that I will regret, or harm others in any way. Come with me, Christ Jesus, as I begin the sacred journey of this day. Amen.

Friday Evening Prayer

Beginning Prayer

Blessed are you, God of sunsets and evening stars. I end this day hoping that I have given you praise and thanksgiving with my whole heart, mind, and soul. You have been with me in all that I have done this day and you will be with me as I sleep. Give me holy rest this night and deep peace. Forgive me for any wrong I have done to you, O God, and to others. Absolve me from the sins I have committed and any good deeds I have omitted.

Bow reverently
R. Holy, holy, holy God, you love me and you forgive me. Blessed, holy, and glorious are you my God, compassionate and loving, this night and forever.

Holy Scripture
(based on Matthew 20:1–16)

Jesus told his followers this parable, "There was a man who owned a large vineyard and he needed workers to harvest his crop. He told his foreman to go out and hire as many people as possible and he would pay them accordingly. The foreman hired workers in the morning and others in the afternoon and still others for the last two hours of the day. But he paid them all the same. The ones who began their work in the morning were angry over this, but the owner said, "I have paid you what we agreed upon. Why do you care if I am generous with those who came at a later hour?"

Praying to Christ

+ I want to be as generous as you, Christ Jesus…

R. Forgive me when I am jealous of the gifts you give others.

+ I want others to be forgiven by you, Christ Jesus…

R. Forgive me when I resent your mercy to others.

+ I want to judge others as you do, Christ Jesus…

R. Help me to be welcoming and compassionate.

Silent Meditation

Bow reverently

Glory be to you, holy, blessed, and glorious Trinity, Father, Son, and Mothering Spirit. I enter now into the silence of your compassionate heart.

Praying with Mary and the Saints

+ Blessed Mother Mary and all you holy angels and saints of God, I join my voice to yours this night as I prepare for my rest…

+ Saint Mark, gospel writer and apostle,

R. Bless those who worked as writers this day.

+ Saint Luke, physician and follower of Christ,

R. Bless those who cared for the sick this day.

+ Saint Margaret Mary Alacoque, religious sister,

R. Bless all who were near the heart of Jesus this day.

+ Saint Elizabeth, cousin and friend to Mary,

R. Bless all pregnant women this day.

Blessed Mary and all you holy angels and saints of God, surround me, bless me, and keep me company this night that I might sleep in God's loving embrace.

Praying with Creation

+ Day and night, sun and clouds, cold and heat, wind and rain, ice and snow…

R. Give praise to God, our holy Creator God.

+ Winter and spring, summer and fall, and all of life's seasons…

R. Give praise to Christ, our holy Savior God.

+ Flowers and trees, meadows and forests, fields and farms, rain forests and deserts…

R. Give praise to the Spirit, our holy Companion God.

All creatures great and small give you praise, O God. May I, too, praise you by striving to be what you have called me to be.

Intercessions

Extend your hands, palms upward

As I end this day, Christ Jesus, I ask your blessing on all your people.

R. Fill them with your devotion and love.

+ Watch over my family members, my friends, my coworkers, and all who have asked for my prayers.

R. Fill them with your devotion and love.

+ Watch over all children this night and may your angels guide their dreams and keep them from fear.

R. Fill them with your devotion and love.

+ Be mindful of laborers the world over this day and bless their rest that they may be renewed for tomorrow.

R. Fill them with your devotion and love.

+ Have mercy on those who are suffering: the sick, the dying, the despairing, the depressed, and carry to yourself all those who have recently died, especially_____.

R. Fill them with your devotion and love.

I pray now in the silence of my heart for these personal intentions...

Ending Prayer

Bow reverently

Holy Savior Jesus, stay with me, for night has come and I want to rest in you. Stay with me, for I want to receive your forgiveness before I sleep. Stay with me, Christ Jesus, as I seek the sacred peace of those who place their trust in you. Amen.

Saturday Morning Prayer

Beginning Prayer

Blessed are you, good and gracious God of sunrises and
morning light. In you I live and move and have my
being; without you I can do nothing. Stir my heart to imitate your compassion, and may I never stray from the
path of your light this day. Be with me now as I join my
sisters and brothers in homes and churches, in convents
and monasteries all over the world in offering you
Saturday morning praise.

Bow reverently
R. Holy, holy, holy God, I rejoice in your love for me. May
I ever praise you; may I ever serve you; may you ever dwell
within my heart. Blessed, holy, and glorious are you, God
of the morning light.

Holy Scripture
(based on 1 Samuel 3:1–10)

When Samuel was a child his parents placed him into the
care of Eli, the high priest of the temple. One night as
Samuel slept, he heard a voice calling him and immediate-
ly he jumped up and ran to Eli. "You called me and here I
am," he said. But Eli said, "I did not call you; go back to
bed." Three times this happened and the third time Eli
understood that God was calling Samuel. And so he
instructed the boy to answer God's call this way: "Here I
am Lord, I am ready to do your will."

Praying to Christ

+ When I forget that you are calling me, Christ Jesus…

R. Remind me to open my heart, my mind, and my spirit to you.

+ When I let the noise of everyday life distract me from your call, Christ Jesus…

R. Remind me to seek you in moments of silent prayer.

+ When I am too preoccupied to listen to you, Christ Jesus…

R. Remind me that without you I can do nothing.

Silent Meditation

Bow reverently

Glory be to you, holy, blessed, and glorious Trinity, Father, Son, and Mothering Spirit. I enter now into the silence of your compassionate heart.

Praying with Mary and the Saints

+ Blessed Mother Mary and all you holy angels and saints of God, I join my voice to yours as I prepare for the work of this day.

+ Saint Stephen, deacon and martyr,

R. Bless those who need great courage this day.

+ Saint Callistus, pope and martyr,

R. Bless all who lead the church this day.

+ Saint Angela Merici, religious and mystic,

R. Bless all who pray for the world this day.

+ Saint Julie Billiart, religious and foundress,

R. Bless all religious women this day.

Blessed Mary and all you holy angels and saints of God,

surround me and challenge me this day to do all that God asks of me with a loving and willing heart.

Praying with Creation

+ Sun and moon, stars and planets, galaxies and endless space…

R. Give praise to God, our holy Creator God.

+ Mountains and valleys, rivers and streams, forests and plains…

R. Give praise to Christ, our holy Savior God.

+ Birds and beasts, fishes and all water creatures, wild animals and household pets…

R. Give praise to the Spirit, our holy Companion God.

All creatures great and small praise you, O God. May I, too, praise you by striving to be all that you have called me to be.

Intercessions

Extend your hands, palms upward

As I begin this new day of life, Christ Jesus, I ask your blessing on all your people the world over.

R. Fill them with the fire of your love.

+ Be with those who travel to work this day and bless their efforts.

R. Fill them with the fire of your love.

+ Watch over all children this day, especially those who are suffering from loneliness and fear.

R. Fill them with the fire of your love.

+ Be mindful of those who work in factories and fields this day and bless the work of their hands.

R. Fill them with the fire of your love.

+ Have mercy on those who are suffering: the sick, the dying, the despairing, the depressed, and carry to yourself all who have recently died, especially_____.

R. Fill them with the fire of your love.

I pray now in the silence of my heart for these personal intentions…

Ending Prayer

Bow reverently

Holy Savior Jesus, I go forth now to practice your love and to share it. Come with me, please, that I may not grow weary. May I do nothing on this Saturday that I will regret, or harm others in any way. Come with me, Christ Jesus, as I begin the sacred journey of this day. Amen.

Saturday Evening Prayer

Beginning Prayer

B lessed are you, God of sunsets and evening stars. I end this day hoping that I have given you praise and thanksgiving with my whole heart, mind, and soul. You have been with me in all that I have done this day and you will be with me as I sleep. Give me holy rest this night and deep peace. Forgive me for any wrong I have done to you, O God, and to others. Absolve me from the sins I have committed and any good deeds I have omitted.

Bow reverently
R. Holy, holy, holy God, you love me and you forgive me. Blessed, holy, and glorious are you, my God, compassionate and loving, this night and forever.

Holy Scripture
(based on John 15:26–27)

Jesus said to his followers, "I will send you the Spirit who comes from the Father and will show you all that is true. The Spirit will help you and remind you of my teachings. Then you will also tell others about me because you have been with me from the beginning."

Praying to Christ

+ I want to receive your Spirit, Christ Jesus…
R. Open my heart to receive this gift.
+ I want to listen to your Spirit, Christ Jesus…

R. Open my ears to hear your teaching.

+ I want to rely on your Spirit for everything, Christ Jesus…

R. Help me to do all that the Spirit asks of me.

Silent Meditation

Bow reverently

Glory be to you, holy, blessed, and glorious Trinity, Father, Son, and Mothering Spirit. I enter now into the silence of your compassionate heart.

Praying with Mary and the Saints

+ Blessed Mother Mary and all you holy angels and saints of God, I join my voice to yours this night as I prepare for my rest…

+ Saint Clement, pope and teacher,

R. Bless those who lead the church this day.

+ Blessed Emmanuel D'Alzon, priest and founder,

R. Bless those in religious life this day.

+ Saint Thomas, apostle and doubter,

R. Bless all who have doubts about God this day.

+ Saint Jude, patron of hopeless causes,

R. Bless all who are in great need this day.

Blessed Mary and all you holy angels and saints of God, surround me, bless me, and keep me company this night that I might rest in God's loving embrace.

Praying with Creation

+ Day and night, sun and clouds, cold and heat, wind and rain, ice and snow…

R. Give praise to God, our holy Creator God.

+ Winter and spring, summer and fall, and all of life's seasons…

R. Give praise to Christ, our holy Savior God.

+ Flowers and trees, meadows and forests, fields and farms, rain forests and deserts…

R. Give praise to the Spirit, our holy Companion God.

All creatures great and small give you praise, O God. May I, too, praise you by striving to be what you have called me to be.

Intercessions

Extend your hands, palms upward

As I end this day, Christ Jesus, I ask your blessing upon all your people the world over.

R. Fill them with your grace and goodness.

+ Watch over me as I sleep and watch over my family members, my friends, my coworkers, and all who have asked for my prayers.

R. Fill them with your grace and goodness.

+ Watch over your children this night and may your angels guide their dreams and keep them from fear.

R. Fill them with your grace and goodness.

+ Be mindful of laborers the world over this day and bless their rest that they may be renewed for their work tomorrow.

R. Fill them with your grace and goodness.

+ Have mercy on those who are suffering: the sick, the dying, the despairing, the depressed, and carry to yourself all those who have recently died, especially_____.

R. Fill them with your grace and goodness.

I pray now in the silence of my heart for these personal intentions…

Ending Prayer

Bow reverently

Holy Savior Jesus, stay with me, for night has come and I want to rest in you. Stay with me, for I need your forgiveness before I sleep. Stay with me, Christ Jesus, as I seek the sacred peace of those who place their trust in you. Amen.

SECTION 2

Prayers for
Special Needs
and Occasions

Prayer of Thanksgiving

Thank you, loving God, Father, Son, and Holy Spirit, for all the blessings you have given me. Thank you for a new day of life, for new possibilities, for new opportunities to serve others. Thank you for my family, my friends, my coworkers, and all who cross my path this day. May I be a sign to all of your great love and care. Thank you, too, for all the big and little surprises that will come my way today. Fill my heart with gratitude and joy. Amen.

For the Gift of Light

Our Father in heaven, thank you for the gift of light in every new day. Thank you, too, for the gift of light that I receive from the people around me. Keep me in your light, away from the darkness of sin and all that makes me less like you. Father of light, help me give light and love to others—as generously as you give them to me. Amen.

Morning Prayer to Mary

Mary, dear and holy mother, I ask for your tender blessing on all those I love. Bless, too, everyone I will encounter this day and all those in need. Ask your son, Jesus, to give me the courage to proclaim his gospel today and to be a witness of his love and mercy in all my words and actions. Teach me, dear mother Mary, how to say "yes" to God in all that I do. Amen.

Prayer for Fathers

Joseph, faithful husband of Mary and foster father of Jesus, I ask your blessing on all fathers this day. May they love and cherish their children and may they be examples of goodness and honesty in all that they do. Bless, too, all who are spiritual fathers: our parish priests, our missionaries, religious brothers, and all who reach out to others with compassion. St. Joseph, pray for me and my loved ones. Amen.

Prayer for Others

Christ Jesus, my Savior and brother, I ask your blessing on all your people. Watch over your children in war-torn lands and where there is famine or drought. Watch over all who have worked to spread the gospel this day and renew them when they are tired or discouraged. Watch over all those who are suffering this day: the sick, the dying, the despairing, and carry to yourself all those who have died. Watch over my family members, my friends, my coworkers, and all who have asked for my prayers this day. Fill us all with your grace and goodness. Amen.

Prayer for Forgiveness

Forgive me, loving savior, Jesus, for any wrong I have done to you or to others this day. Pardon me if I have not done my best at home and at work. Absolve me from the sins I have committed or any good deeds I have omitted. I know that you love and forgive me, and I welcome your healing grace. I ask your forgiveness, too, for all the sins of your people throughout the world. Give all of us your healing peace that we may come to know you and your compassionate heart. Amen.

Prayer for Peace

Holy God, I ask you to give peace to our world. I believe it is your desire that people live together in harmony and mutual respect. But human limitation, greed, and hatred pave the way for war. Strengthen those who are working for peace and heal those who have been wounded by war, especially the innocent victims. Pour your healing grace on all your children all over the world that we might be peacemakers in all our words and actions. Grant us your peace, O God. Amen.

During an Illness

Loving God, please be at my side during this illness. Hold my hand in my pain and forgive me when I am impatient or unduly afraid. Cure me if you want to and when you can. I love you and I know that you are with me always. Help me be brave and not inflict my suffering on others. Thank you for the gift of medication that eases my pain. I ask your blessing on all who suffer this day. Amen.

Prayer for Deceased Loved Ones

Dear God, I remember this day all those close to me who have died. May they know the healing and comfort of your merciful love. Bless me, too, this day that my aching heart may be healed. I miss my loved ones and it is not the same without them. Help me recall the good they have done and imitate it. Thank you for the gift of having known and loved them. Amen.

Prayer for the Sick

I ask your blessing, Divine Physician, on all who are sick this day. Bless those who have no doctor to treat them or medication to ease their pain. Bless those who are in hospitals that they might bear their suffering with dignity. Bless those who have a terminal illness that they might be comforted with your grace and healed in spirit. Bless those who are mentally ill or suffering from emotional disorders; may they and all who are sick know your healing and be at peace. Amen.

Prayer in Times of Terror

I ask you, God of peace and goodness, to help our country as it deals with the shock and pain of terror. Heal those who have suddenly lost loved ones, and strengthen those who risk their lives to protect others. Though I don't understand sin and evil or why anyone would inflict violence on innocent victims, help me have courage in the face of terror and place my faith in you. Watch over us and heal us, loving God, and be near us in our pain. Amen.

Prayer to the Prince of Peace

Jesus, Prince of Peace, without you we walk in darkness and conflict. Send your Spirit into our hearts that we might turn away from the darkness of sin and hatred and seek peace and justice for all. Bless and inspire our world leaders to work for peace and to turn away from war and violence. Bless all the people in our world who are the tragic victims of war. Bless our young people in a special way that they might turn away from all forms of violence. Please help them and heal them that they might experience your gift of peace in their hearts. Amen.

Prayer for a Sick Family Member

Jesus, Great Healer, I come before you today to ask your blessing on all who are sick. I ask in particular that you place your healing hand on _____ that he/she might be cured. I believe that all things are possible with you and that you want only good things for us. If it be your holy will, give my loved one relief from illness, peace of mind, and the courage to accept whatever he/she must endure this day. Amen.

For Our World Leaders

Son of God, you are lord of lords and king of kings. You are the first and the last. We come before you, then, to ask your blessing on our world leaders, and especially on our president, the members of Congress, and on our state and local leaders. Give them wisdom and humility that they might put God's will and the good of God's children before all else. Help them act unselfishly for the sake of justice, freedom, and peace for all peoples. Give them patience and goodness that they might follow God's way and not their own. May they rule as you do, always for the good of others. Amen.

For Doing God's Will

Loving God, I cannot live without you. Help me think and act rightly that I might always live as you would have me live. Teach me to recognize your holy will, to search it out, and then to follow it with all my mind, heart, body, and soul. If I should stray from the path you have set for me, direct me, loving God, and show me the way. Holy God, mighty God, may I live as you would have me live this day and always. Amen.

For a Difficult Decision

Jesus, beloved Savior, please give me your light and grace that I might see my way through this difficult decision. Guide me as I weigh the possibilities, and help me to keep the needs of those I love clearly in view. Help me keep God's will for me in view as well, that whatever I do, I might be walking on the path to God. Give me wisdom and understanding, please; give me patience and courage, dear Savior, that I might be guided by your light and your light alone. Come Holy Spirit, come and help me in this difficult time. Amen.

For Growing Spiritually

Lord Jesus Christ, by your saving death and resurrection, free me from my sins and weaknesses. Help me reach out to others in love and service and search out God's will in the daily activities of my day. May I always put the needs of others before my own. May I so love my family, friends, and coworkers that they will see only your grace in me. May your love and your light shine through everything I do. Amen.

Prayer for Healing

Dear God, I need your healing touch this day. I get so impatient with my aches and pains, with a body that can't do all the things I want it to. Help me, please, to place myself in your care and let your strength sustain me. Help me quiet my heart, silence my fears, and rest in you. I pray, too, for all your children who are suffering from an illness this day. Give them comfort and healing that they may go forward on the path you have set for them. May my suffering and theirs be united to the suffering of your son on the cross. Amen.

In Thanksgiving for Surprises

O God of Surprises, every day is fresh and new and filled with wonderful discoveries. Every day holds mysteries to be unfolded and life-secrets to be discovered. Help me be open this day to whatever surprises you have in store for me. Help me see each moment of living as gift, each personal encounter as wonder-filled, and each aspect of your creation as miracle. May I never take your goodness for granted, and may I be open to all the wonderful things you have in store for me. Amen.

SECTION 3

Seasonal
Prayers

All Saints Day

All you holy saints of God, we join our prayers of praise to yours this day. With you, we sing of God's goodness, rejoice in God's mercy, and celebrate God's incredible love. Teach us to live as you lived—always thinking of others, always recognizing our weakness, always rejoicing in God's gifts, always closely following Jesus. Blessed are you, happy are you, all you holy saints of God. Pray for us that someday we too may be among God's holy ones. Amen.

All Souls Day

Jesus, dear Savior, on this day we prayerfully remember all our loved ones who have died. Please give them comfort and hope, and may they be at peace, knowing that they will soon rest in God's arms eternally. Thank you for our memories of them and for all the good times we shared. We ask you, please, through their intercession, to deepen our faith, strengthen our hope, and increase our love that we, too, may someday stand before you ready to enter your holy Kingdom. Amen.

Thanksgiving Day

Great Creator God, giver of all good things, we rejoice in the harvest of your blessings. We thank you for children and spouses, for family and friends, for food and drink, for hearth and home, for the gifts of faith, hope, and love, and for all your spiritual gifts. We ask your blessing on those among us who hunger and thirst, who are homeless and alone, who need your guiding hand, and who depend on your tender mercy. Great Creator God, we praise your holy name on this Thanksgiving Day and always. Amen.

For Advent Blessings

Come Lord Jesus, come Emmanuel, come and rest in our hearts this Advent season. Teach us to be generous in our giving and generous with our time and attention. May we await you with peaceful hearts, with hearts that yearn for you as our greatest and most cherished gift. In all our preparations for Christmas, may we keep our eyes on you, knowing and believing that you alone are the reason we celebrate. Be born again in us, dear Savior, that we might reflect your love and goodness to everyone we meet in this time of Advent.

Come Lord Jesus, come Emmanuel, come and rest in our hearts. Amen.

For the Advent Journey

As we begin our Advent journey, dear God of Love, help us to recognize the great gift you have given us in Jesus. On each day of this journey, may we move closer to him, the Prince of peace, the Light of the world. In all our preparations for Christmas, may we always remember that Jesus is the reason for this blessed season. Thank you, loving God, for this time of joy and expectation. Walk with us and show us the way today and every day of Advent. Amen.

Christmas Prayer

Come, Lord Jesus, Light of world, Prince of peace and beloved Savior; come into our hearts this Christmas and fill us with your gifts of love and joy. Thank you for "gifting" us with your presence among us. With Mary and Joseph, we rejoice and thank God for you. With the angels and saints we sing, "Glory to God in the highest." With the Magi and the shepherds we bow before you with hearts full of wonder. Dear Emmanuel, God with us, help us to follow you faithfully and to share the good news of your coming with everyone we meet. Amen.

Prayer for the Easter Season

On this day, loving and gracious God, we praise and bless you for raising Jesus from the dead. We praise and bless you, too, for all the times you have raised us up through your grace. When we are weak and unable to make good decisions; when we are stubborn and refuse to forgive others; when we are afraid or discouraged and forget that you strengthen us, raise us up, loving God, raise us up. Thank you for giving us new life in Jesus and for his presence among us. Amen.

Pentecost Prayer

Come, Holy Spirit, Spirit of the Risen Christ, fill us with the abundance of your grace. May we be open to the gifts you so generously give us: wisdom, understanding, knowledge, awe, courage, true spirituality, and openness. Strengthen us when we are needy and weak, too afraid to take risks and speak out when we should. Divine Counselor, be with us and bless us on this Day of Pentecost and always. Amen.

Scripture-Based Prayers

For Holy Fear and Great Joy

May I come looking for you, risen Christ, as the women in the gospel did. Give me, please, the same holy fear and great joy that they experienced, so I might know your peace in my heart. Then, having your peace, may I reach out to my family, friends, and coworkers to generously share it. Amen.   *Matthew 28:8–15*

For Faith and Persistence

Holy Spirit, Spirit of the living Christ, fill my heart today with your gifts of faith and persistence. May I believe that you dwell in my heart and may I continue to look for the signs of your presence all around me: at home, at work, in my neighborhood, and everywhere I go this day. Amen.

John 20:11–18

For a Burning Heart

Jesus, risen Savior, walk with me today as you walked with the disciples on the road to Emmaus. Be with me on the "road" to work, to school, to appointments, to meetings, to practices, and back home again. Give me the grace to listen for you and to recognize you and to feel my heart burning within me because of you. Amen.

Luke 24:13–35

For Faith in Action

Through my baptism, loving Savior, I have proclaimed myself your follower. Help me to live my Catholic faith, not just on Sundays, but every moment of my life. Help me to be open to the times you speak to me through others and guide me as I try to live your gospel message. Amen. *Mark 16:9–15*

For the Gift of Jesus

Loving God, thank you for calling me to faith. Thank you for the gift of Jesus who walks with me, whether I "see" him or not. Help my faith to deepen, and when I have doubts, help me to believe that Jesus understands and perhaps even smiles at me. Keep your guiding hand on me this day. Amen. *John 20:19–31*

For Understanding

Loving Savior, I, like Nicodemus, am slow to understand all that you want to tell me. I look for answers that I can process with my human intellect, in spite of all the times you have reminded me that faith cannot be grasped with the intellect alone. Strengthen my faith in you, Jesus, and continue to teach me in spite of my resistance. Amen.

John 3:7–15

For the Gift of Enlightenment

Jesus, you are the light of the world. Teach me how to walk in the light and never to choose the darkness of sin and selfishness. Help me, too, to be a light for those who depend on me. May they see your light and goodness in my acts of love and care. Jesus, light of the world, pray for me. Amen.

John 3:16–21

For an Open Heart

I need you in my life, blessed Savior. I forget to tell you so, and I forget to invite you into my heart. May the example of your disciples on the road to Emmaus inspire me to invite you more often, not just as night falls but always. Open my heart and mind to hear your words and to delight in your presence as your disciples did. Amen.

Luke 24:13–35

For Fidelity

I choose you again today, Jesus, to be my companion, my spiritual leader. I place my faith in you and your teachings. Help me to follow you faithfully at home, at work, in all my dealings with others this day. "To whom else could I go, for you have the words of eternal life." Amen.

John 6:60–69

For Transformation

Take my heart of darkness, Jesus, and transform it into a heart of light and goodness. Strengthen my faith that I might rely on you and follow your guiding light. Rescue me from the darkness of doubt and fear that I might believe in your unending light. Amen.

John 12:44–50

For Greater Love

With Peter I proclaim, Christ Jesus: "You know that I love you." In spite of my weakness and failures, I do love you and I do want to "feed your lambs" in whatever ways I can. Walk with me this day and show me the way to give witness to you. Amen.   *John 21:15–19*

For the Church

I rejoice in your abiding presence, Holy Spirit, and I thank you for dwelling within your church. You know how much we need you. You know how weak and misguided your church can be. Shed the light of your grace upon us today, just as you gave it to the followers of Jesus as they awaited your coming in tongues of fire and blowing wind. Come, Holy Spirit, dwell within us. Amen.

John 20:19–23

Traditional
Prayers

The Lord's Prayer

Our Father who art in heaven,
hallowed be Thy name.
Thy kingdom come. Thy will be done
on earth as it is in Heaven.
Give us this day our daily bread,
and forgive us our trespasses,
as we forgive those who trespass against us,
and lead us not into temptation,
but deliver us from evil. Amen.

Hail Mary

Hail Mary, full of grace, the Lord is with thee;
blessed art thou among women, and blessed is the fruit of
thy womb, Jesus. Holy Mary, mother of God, pray for us
sinners, now and at the hour of our death. Amen.

Glory Be

Glory be to the Father and to the Son and to the Holy
Spirit, as it was in the beginning, is now, and will be
forever. Amen.

Prayer for Faith, Hope, and Love

I believe, O Lord; may I believe yet more firmly.
I trust in you, O Lord; may I trust you yet more firmly.
I love you, O Lord; may I love you yet more deeply. Guide
me by your wisdom. Comfort me by your mercy. Protect
me by your power. May I always deal fairly with my neighbors, and be courageous in the face of danger. May I be
patient in my trials and humble in my successes. May I
ever be joyful in all things. Amen.

A Prayer of Praise

(based on the Gloria at Mass)

Glory to you, God most high; please give peace to your
people on earth. We worship you and we give you thanks.
We praise you, Lord Jesus Christ. You are the lamb of God
who takes away the sin of the world. Have mercy on us
and hear our prayers. You are God's holy one, God's exalt-
ed one, Lord Jesus. Send us your Holy Spirit this day and
always. Amen.

A Prayer of Contrition

(based on the Confiteor at Mass)

I confess to you, loving and almighty God, and to all my
brothers and sisters, that I have sinned through my own
fault, in my thoughts and in my words, in what I have
done, and in what I have failed to do. I ask blessed Mary
and all your angels and saints to pray for me that I might
turn to you with all my heart, mind, and soul. Amen.

Prayer to the Holy Spirit

Come, Holy Spirit, fill the hearts of your faithful people and enkindle in them the fire of your love. Come among us and we shall be renewed; come among us and renew the face of the earth. O God, by the light of the Holy Spirit you have taught us your ways. May the Spirit always guide us toward what is right and remind us often of your love and care. We ask these things in the name of Christ Jesus. Amen.

Mary's Song of Praise

My whole being proclaims your greatness, O God, my spirit rejoices in you, God my Savior. You have looked with favor on me, a simple servant. Yet, from this day on, all generations will call me blessed because of the great things you have done for me. Holy is your name. You show mercy to those who honor you, from generation to generation. You show strength by putting the proud in their place and pushing the mighty from their thrones. You lift up those who are humble and small; you fill the hungry with good things, and you send the rich away empty-handed. You forever come to the assistance of your chosen ones, just as you promised Abraham and his children. Yes, my whole being proclaims your greatness, O God, and my spirit rejoices in you.

Memorare

Remember, most loving Virgin Mary,
never was it heard
that anyone who turned to you for help
was left unaided.
Inspired by this confidence,
though burdened by my sins,
I turn to your protection
for you are my mother.
Mother of the Word of God,
do not dismiss my words of pleading
but be merciful and hear my prayer.
Amen.

The Apostles' Creed

I believe in God, the Father almighty,
creator of heaven and earth.
I believe in Jesus Christ, his only Son, our Lord.
He was conceived by the power of the Holy Spirit
and born of the Virgin Mary.
He suffered under Pontius Pilate,
was crucified, died, and was buried.
He descended to the dead.
On the third day he rose again.
He ascended into heaven,
and is seated at the right hand of the Father.
He will come again to judge the living and the dead.
I believe in the Holy Spirit,
the holy Catholic church,
the communion of saints,
the forgiveness of sins,
the resurrection of the body,
and life everlasting. Amen.

Angelus

V. The angel of the Lord declared unto Mary

R. And she conceived of the Holy Spirit.

Hail Mary, full of grace...

V. Behold the handmaid of the Lord.

R. Be it done unto me according to your word

Hail Mary, full of grace...

V. And the Word was made flesh,

R. And dwelt among us.

Hail Mary, full of grace...

V. Pray for us, O holy Mother of God,

R. That we may be made worthy of the promises of
Christ.

Let us pray. Pour forth we beseech you, O Lord,
your grace into our hearts; that we,

to whom the Incarnation of Christ your Son,

was made known by the message of an angel,

may by his passion and cross

be brought to the glory of his resurrection.

We ask this through the same Christ, our Lord. Amen.

Hail Holy Queen (Salve Regina)

Hail holy queen, mother of mercy,
you are our life, our sweetness, and our hope.
To you we cry, the children of Eve,
To you we send up our sighs,
mourning and weeping in this land of exile.
Turn, then most gracious mother
your eyes of mercy toward us.
Lead us home at last and show us
the blessed fruit of your womb, Jesus:
O clement, O loving, O sweet Virgin Mary.

Blessing before Meals

Bless us, O Lord, and these your gifts
which we are about to receive
from your goodness,
through Christ Our Lord. Amen.

Prayers to and by the Saints

The Peace Prayer

Lord, make me an instrument of your peace.
Where there is hatred, let me sow love;
Where there is injury, pardon;
Where there is doubt, faith;
Where there is despair, hope;
Where there is darkness, light;
Where there is sadness, joy.
O divine Master, grant that I may not so much seek
To be consoled, as to console,
To be understood, as to understand,
To be loved, as to love,
For it is in giving that we receive;
In pardoning that we are pardoned;
It is in dying that we are born to eternal life.

Attributed to Saint Francis of Assisi

Prayer to Saint Peter

Jesus called you the rock, Saint Peter, even though you
denied him three times. He trusted you to lead his followers and to give witness to his gospel. Pray for us please
and help us to rise from our failures and our faithlessness.
May we know, as you did, the power of Jesus' forgiving
love and compassion, and may we be disciples who daily
give witness to our faith. Amen.

Prayer to Saint Paul

Saint Paul, apostle and teacher, pray that we might be faithful followers of Jesus, especially by showing love and respect for one another. May the fire that burned in your heart burn in our hearts too. Pray for us, Saint Paul, that we might be grateful for the gift of our faith and gladly share it with others. May the fire that burned in your heart burn in our hearts too. Amen.

For a Holy Heart

Lord, grant me a holy heart
that sees always what is fine and pure
and is not frightened at the sight of sin,
but creates order wherever it goes.
Grant me a heart that knows nothing
of boredom, weeping, and sighing.
Let me not be too concerned
with the bothersome thing
I call myself.
Lord, give me a sense of humor
and I will find happiness in life
and profit for others.   *Saint Thomas More*

Prayer to the Holy Spirit

Breathe in me, O Holy Spirit, that my thoughts may all be holy. Act in me, O Holy Spirit, that my work, too, may be holy. Draw my heart, O Holy Spirit, that I might love only what is holy. Strengthen me, O Holy Spirit, to defend all that is holy. Guard me, then, O Holy Spirit, that I always may be holy. Amen. *Saint Augustine*

Prayer for Faith

Jesus Christ, beloved Savior and Brother, my prayer is that you will open the eyes of all who believe in you that we might see the wonders you place before us. Through your Holy Spirit, you are always with us, guiding, encouraging, leading forth, but we don't know what a wondrous grace this is. Your Spirit groans within us, praying for us in words we cannot express ourselves, but we don't know what a wondrous grace this is. Your Spirit puts in our daily path surprises and miracles even, but we don't know what a wondrous grace this is. You have promised to be with us always that we may be joyful as we follow your gospel way, but we don't know what a wondrous grace this is. We are on a sacred path to God with the Holy Spirit as our mentor and guide, but we don't know what a wondrous grace this is. Open our eyes of faith, O Christ, that we might respond with all our hearts to all that you so generously give us. Amen. *In the Spirit of Pope John XXIII*

Prayer to Saint Joseph

Saint Joseph, model of all who are devoted to labor, help me to work conscientiously by placing love of duty above my own inclinations; to gratefully and joyously deem it an honor to use and develop the gifts I have received from God, to work steadily and peacefully and with moderation and patience, without ever shrinking from the work I am called to do. Pray for me, Saint Joseph, that my work might give glory and honor to God. Amen. *Based on a prayer by Saint Pius X*

Prayer for Courage

Lord, almighty God, Father of your beloved and blessed Son Jesus Christ, through whom we have come to know you, God of angels, of powers, of all creation, of all the saints who live in your sight, I bless you for judging me worthy of this day, this hour, so that in the company of the martyrs I may share the cup of Christ, your anointed one. With your grace may I rise to eternal life in soul and body, immortal through the power of the Holy Spirit. May I be received among the martyrs in your presence today as a rich and pleasing sacrifice. I praise you for all things, I bless you, and I glorify you now and forever. Amen.

Based on a prayer by Saint Polycarp
(before he was martyred)

Prayer for Youth

Lord, Jesus Christ, I ask your blessing on our young people today. May they respond to you with strong and generous hearts. May they offer their youth and generous enthusiasm to proclaim your gospel in our world. May they be salt and light to every person they encounter and may they answer your call with joy and give their lives in loving service to all their brothers and sisters. Just as you trust in them, Christ Jesus, may they also place their trust in you. Amen.   *Pope John Paul II*

Prayer before Communion

Gracious God of majesty and awe,
I seek your protection,
I look for your healing.
I cannot bear your judgment,
but I trust in your salvation.
Lord Jesus Christ,
look upon me with mercy and hear my prayer,
for I trust in you.
Have mercy on me,
for I am full of sorrow and sin.
I open my heart to receive you,
relying solely on your
forgiveness and compassion. Amen.

Communion prayer of Saint Ambrose (adapted)

Prayer to Saint Anthony of Padua

Holy Saint Anthony, gentle and powerful in your help, miracles waited on your word, which you were always ready to request for those in trouble or anxiety. Encouraged by this thought, I implore you to obtain for me (request). You are the saint of miracles, gentle and loving Saint Anthony. Your heart is ever full of human sympathy, and I know that you will take my petition to the Infant Savior for whom you have such a great love. The gratitude of my heart will ever be yours. Amen.

Prayer to Saint Blaise

O glorious Saint Blaise, by your martyrdom you left the church a precious witness to the faith. Obtain for us, we pray, the grace to preserve within ourselves this divine gift of faith and to show by our words and example the truth of that same faith. You once miraculously cured a little child at the point of death from an affliction of the throat, and so we ask for your powerful protection in like misfortunes. Above all, help us to cling to the wisdom of the gospel and to be sorry for our sins and failings. Amen.

Prayer to Saint John Bosco

O glorious Saint John Bosco, you were called by God to work with youth and to mould them in the light of faith and Christian morality. You sacrificed yourself to the very end of your life to offer them safety, happiness, and education. May we, too, have a holy love for our young people today who are exposed to so many temptations. Keep them safe from the dangers of the world, and guide them on the sacred path that leads to God. Amen.

Prayer to Saint Jude

Saint Jude, patron of hopeless cases, I pray through your intercession, for all people who are suffering from depression or anxiety, for all who are suffering from disease and hunger, for all who are suffering from the spiritual and physical pain of cancer, AIDs, or other terminal illnesses. Though our need is great, we rely on your intercession with Christ Jesus for healing of heart, mind, and body if it be God's will. Amen.

Prayer to Saint Martin de Porres

Saint Martin de Porres, we unite our prayer to yours as we pray for unity and peace among all the peoples of the world. You yourself were the victim of prejudice and hate and you devoted yourself to caring for the least ones of Christ. Saint Martin, may we, through your example, treat all others with dignity and compassion. May we, in our imitation of you, show people of every race and every color the path to unity and justice. Amen.

Prayer of Consolation

Let nothing disturb you, nothing frighten you;
all things are passing, God never changes!
Patient endurance leads to all good things;
Those whom God possesses want for nothing;
God alone suffices.   *Saint Teresa of Avila*

Prayer for God's Support

May God support us all the day long till the shadows lengthen and the evening comes and the busy world is hushed and the fever of life is over and our work is done.

Then in mercy may God give us a safe lodging and a holy rest and peace at last.

John Henry Cardinal Newman

To Do God's Will

O my God, I ask of you for myself and for those whom I hold dear, the grace to fulfill perfectly your holy will, to accept for love of you the joys and sorrows of this passing life, so that we may one day be united in Heaven for all eternity.   *Saint Thérèse of Lisieux*

Stations of the Cross

Stations of the Cross

It is an honored tradition in the church to walk the path that Jesus followed from the courtroom of Pontius Pilate to the place where he died. In Jerusalem this path is today called the "Via Dolorosa" or the Sorrowful Way. Certain spots where Jesus stopped along this route are marked, and these are called "stations."

Over the centuries many people traveled to Jerusalem to retrace and recall Jesus' steps to Calvary, especially during Lent. But Jerusalem was too far for most people. So, in the Middle Ages they began making this "journey" in churches using painted or carved images of the fourteen stops Jesus made. At each station people would recall what happened to Jesus and pray about it.

Today many people continue to reflect and pray in the company of Jesus along the "Sorrowful Way," and not just in churches and not just during Lent. The stations that follow here are meant to be prayed anywhere and anytime all year long.

Introduction

When Jesus issues the invitation, "Come, follow me," he is speaking to real people like us. He wants us to follow him with heart, mind, soul, and body. And just as Jesus felt pain, frustration, and deep emotional hurts, so will we in our daily lives as Christians.

When we pray the Way of the Cross, we have the opportunity to unite ourselves to Jesus and to reflect on his sufferings—and on our own. But we also have the opportunity to witness the tremendous love Jesus had for others: for Pilate who judged him falsely, for the soldiers who were abusive, for Simon the reluctant helper, for the women who wept so openly, and indeed for ourselves, too, for whom Jesus prayed from the cross, "Father, forgive them…."

Jesus teaches us that there is no greater love than to give ourselves for others. He teaches us, too, that when we "die" daily in loving service, resurrection will follow. This is what our Christian life is all about. Though we sometimes sow in sorrow, we can always reap with joy. Why? Because we are followers of Jesus, and he is always with us to guide us. Let us go forth now in his footsteps.

First Station

Pilate Condemns Jesus

Pilate, the judge, did not know Jesus personally. On the word of others, he passed judgment on him. Jesus was at the mercy of this aloof Roman official, this stranger, and yet he did not protest. He was defenseless and vulnerable, and yet he accepted the situation for what it was.

Personal Reflection

I am a follower of Jesus. I offer my time, my talent, and my energy to my family, my job, my friends, and my neighbors. But I am sometimes "condemned" by people who don't know me personally. I am held responsible when there are problems that are beyond my expertise or control. I am sometimes defenseless and vulnerable—as Jesus was.

Prayer

Jesus, you are my example. You did not try to defend yourself; you did not make excuses. Your love overcame your need to do so. Help me love those I encounter daily, to stop making excuses for myself, and to put the needs of others before my own. Teach me how to follow you.

Silent Meditation

Spend a few minutes praying silently about the needs and concerns of family members, coworkers, friends, and your brothers and sisters throughout the world.

Second Station
Jesus Carries His Cross

It was decided that Jesus should die, and the instrument of his death was thrust upon his shoulders. He was pushed forward by the soldiers with curses and jeers. Where were all those people he had blessed and taught and healed?

Personal Reflection

I am a follower of Jesus. I am blessing and teaching daily when I do my very best as a parent, employee, and friend. More often than not I do this without thanks or praise. But I continue to do it because I believe that to follow Christ is the most important thing in my life.

Prayer

Jesus, I can't help wanting thanks and praise for the good things I do. I want my children and spouse to at least say thank you; I want my boss to acknowledge the key role I play at work, and I want my coworkers to admire and thank me. Help me not to look for rewards, but to dedicate myself to serving the needs of others—as you have called me to do. Teach me how to follow you.

Silent Meditation

Spend a few minutes praying silently about the needs and concerns of family members, coworkers, friends, and your brothers and sisters throughout the world.

Third Station

Jesus Falls the First Time

Far too much was demanded of Jesus. The weight of the wooden beam was too heavy. He fell to the ground in front of the crowd. Some probably even cheered this sign of weakness in one who had seemed so strong.

Personal Reflection

I am a follower of Jesus. Sometimes too much is demanded of me, and so I fall. My family and friends make demands. My boss and coworkers make demands—especially on my time and patience. My burden is heavy, and I don't always carry it well.

Prayer

Jesus, the hardest thing of all for me is dealing with my own expectations. As long as I think that it's up to me to change others for the better, all by myself, I am going to fail. I am going to "fall." Help me remember you at these times. You were able to accept people as they were. Help me accept my family, my coworkers, my neighbors—as they are—and accept my own limitations. Teach me how to follow you.

Silent Meditation

Spend a few minutes praying silently about the needs and concerns of family members, coworkers, friends, and your brothers and sisters throughout the world.

Fourth Station

Jesus Meets His Mother

Mary wanted the best for Jesus. She wanted others to applaud him, to like him, to marvel at the wonder of him. And yet, here she meets him as a public failure, carrying the cross for his own crucifixion.

Personal Reflection

I am a follower of Jesus. Sometimes it's very difficult to watch my children fail. I teach them, I correct them, and I say the same things over and over. I love them and I want the best for them. Still they sometimes fail. I don't want to give up on them. I want to believe that resurrection is a real possibility in their lives.

Prayer

Jesus, Mary was well aware that people in the crowd considered you a failure. In some small way I can appreciate how she felt. I hate it when my children don't do well in school or don't respect the rights of others. I want everyone to think that I'm doing a great job, but it doesn't always happen that way. It didn't happen that way for your mother either. Teach me how to follow you.

Silent Meditation

Spend a few minutes praying silently about the needs and concerns of family members, coworkers, friends, and your brothers and sisters throughout the world.

Fifth Station

Simon Helps Jesus

Jesus encounters Simon, the reluctant one. Simon probably didn't come forward freely; he probably didn't want to get involved with Jesus at all. He was dragged into it. Quite possibly this encounter changed Simon's life forever, but Scripture doesn't spell this out for us.

Personal Reflection

I am a follower of Jesus. I know only too well how it feels to encounter "reluctant ones" even in my own family. They seem to close their minds and hearts to the gospel way of life, but I can't be sure. And so I worry about them and I pray for them. Sometimes I myself am one of the reluctant ones. It's not easy to pick up the cross with Jesus.

Prayer

Jesus, I can't help wondering about Simon. Was he a better person because he met you? Are my children, spouse, coworkers, friends, better because they encounter me? I am sorry that I am sometimes a reluctant witness and sometimes even a poor one. I need your sustaining grace. Teach me how to follow you.

Silent Meditation

Spend a few minutes praying silently about the needs and concerns of family members, coworkers, friends, and your brothers and sisters throughout the world.

Sixth Station

Veronica Offers Comfort

Veronica was oblivious to personal danger. She sprang forward to comfort and cleanse Jesus with a soothing cloth! She didn't care about the soldiers; she only saw the blood and the sweat on the face of Jesus, who had so often loved and cared for others.

Personal Reflection

I am a follower of Jesus. He has told me clearly in Scripture that when I do something for his least ones, his little ones, I do it for him. Can I dare to be a Veronica for those others, holding out to them the cloth of love, forgiveness, and compassion?

Prayer

Jesus, I spend far too much time worrying about what others will think of me. I am so intent on being the perfect parent, employee, spouse, and friend that I fail to notice the needs of others. Help me understand their struggles and their frustrations so I can continue to hold out to them the cloth of care and comfort. Teach me how to follow you.

Silent Meditation

Spend a few minutes praying silently about the needs and concerns of family members, coworkers, friends, and your brothers and sisters throughout the world.

Seventh Station

Jesus Falls Again

Jesus was overburdened by the weight of the cross, but he was left to fend for himself. Couldn't the soldiers have helped him up? Couldn't someone from the crowd have come forward? Surely there was at least one person there whom Jesus had helped. Where was that person now?

Personal Reflection

I am a follower of Jesus. I sometimes feel overburdened by life and all its demands. Yet I still hope to be a good role model, a good Christian. There are so many times when it seems to me that I get no guidance or support from others. In this situation wouldn't Jesus have picked himself up and moved forward? Can I do less?

Prayer

Jesus, I feel so sorry for myself at times. I get discouraged when I fail to keep up with all the demands on my time and energy. I get annoyed when others take advantage of me. Help me imitate you. Even when you knew you were heading toward Calvary, you picked yourself up and moved on. Teach me how to follow you.

Silent Meditation

Spend a few minutes praying silently about the needs and concerns of family members, coworkers, friends, and your brothers and sisters throughout the world.

Eighth Station

Jesus Meets the Women

Those mysterious women of Jerusalem! They were weeping and wailing at the sight of Jesus. Why did he rebuke them? Why didn't he welcome their grief? Were they perhaps crying because they wanted attention or because it was a social custom? Jesus told them to cry for themselves and their children. Did he think they were shedding false tears?

Personal Reflection

I am a follower of Jesus. And yet I have a kinship with those women. Don't I often feel like weeping and wailing when things don't go my way? I am weeping for myself, of course; I am feeling sorry for myself. Perhaps my tears should be for the times when I have failed to give witness to the love, truth, and peace that Jesus offers.

Prayer

Jesus, I wonder what you would say to me about my self-pity. It's so easy for me to blame everyone else. I weep for myself—and you see right through me. Help me re-dedicate myself to you and to everyone in my life who depends on me. Teach me how to follow you.

Silent Meditation

Spend a few minutes praying silently about the needs and concerns of family members, coworkers, friends, and your brothers and sisters throughout the world.

Ninth Station

Jesus Falls Once Again

Jesus fell for the third time. Why was he forced to stumble along this way? Did the soldiers enjoy inflicting torture? Was the crowd enjoying the fact that someone who had been so well known and so self-assured was now so humiliated?

Personal Reflection

I am a follower of Jesus. From day to day I stumble along, sometimes failing miserably. No one comes forward to help. Why not? Maybe I am unconsciously hiding my need for support because I don't want to admit failure. If Jesus would have accepted help, why won't I?

Prayer

Jesus, when I make a mistake with one of my children, it would do me so much good to sit down with other parents to get their advice. But this would be an admission on my part that I can't handle my own problems. Is that so bad? Why do I insist upon stumbling along? Give me the courage to break this pattern, to admit my needs, and to rely on others. Teach me how to follow you.

Silent Meditation

Spend a few minutes praying silently about the needs and concerns of family members, coworkers, friends, and your brothers and sisters throughout the world.

Tenth Station
Jesus Was Stripped

Jesus was stripped of everything he owned, even his clothing. He was helpless against the cruelty of the soldiers, and he must have been humiliated by their disgraceful treatment. He had given so much to others and this is what he got in return.

Personal Reflection

I am a follower of Jesus. There are times when I, too, feel stripped—stripped of power to make decisions, stripped of patience when I most need it, stripped of time because of so many demands. I know that these deprivations are nothing compared to what Jesus endured. And yet, I need courage to bear them.

Prayer

Jesus, I am ashamed to admit that I want praise and thanks for what I give to others. I expect my children to "do me proud"; I want coworkers to thank me for a job well done. I want my boss to admire and compliment my accomplishments. Help me to learn from you to accept life as it really is and to accept myself as I really am. Teach me how to follow you.

Silent Meditation

Spend a few minutes praying silently about the needs and concerns of family members, coworkers, friends, and your brothers and sisters throughout the world.

Eleventh Station

Jesus Was Nailed to the Cross

Jesus was pushed and prodded and then thrown down to be nailed to the cross. He was just one more body for the soldiers to deal with. After a lifetime of giving to others, how must it have felt to be treated in this harsh and unfair way?

Personal Reflection

I am a follower of Jesus. I offer my time and my talents—not consciously looking for great financial or personal rewards. And yet, how it hurts when my contributions are not acknowledged, when people take advantage of me, or worse yet, when they criticize me for things over which I have no control. What can I learn from the response of Jesus?

Prayer

Jesus, how can I compare my own daily ups and downs with the tremendous pain you bore? Yet I know that you understand and forgive me even when I am less than generous with my time and attention to those who need me. I need to learn from you how to give with selfless love. Teach me how to follow you.

Silent Meditation

Spend a few minutes praying silently about the needs and concerns of family members, coworkers, friends, and your brothers and sisters throughout the world.

Twelfth Station

Jesus Dies on the Cross

The moment of death on the cross was filled with pain for Jesus. The physical pain was excruciating, but the mental pain must have been even worse. He had heard the call of God and he had followed it. He had gone without rest, often without food and drink, to teach and to serve others. Where are all those others now?

Personal Reflection

I am a follower of Jesus. I want to imitate the way he gave of himself without complaining or making others feel guilty for taking his time and attention. I want to be a loving and caring parent, spouse, coworker, and friend, but too often I hold back; I don't give without counting the cost.

Prayer

Jesus, there have been people in my life for whom I have bent over backwards. I have given them love and attention often expecting something in return. You gave without counting the cost and I want to be like you. I want to give of myself more generously. Teach me how to follow you.

Silent Meditation

Spend a few minutes praying silently about the needs and concerns of family members, coworkers, friends, and your brothers and sisters throughout the world.

Thirteenth Station

Jesus is Taken Down

When Jesus was taken down from the cross, he was placed in the arms of his mother. Without concern for the blood and sweat and dirt on his body, she gathered him to herself. What helpless and agonizing sorrow she must have felt.

Personal Reflection

I am a follower of Jesus. I am called to hold out my arms to many others in the course of a day. I am called to receive them in my embrace, even when they make too many demands on me. What helplessness I sometimes feel! I have to remember to look to Mary for strength and guidance.

Prayer

Jesus, I admire your mother so much. She must have been a warm and wonderful woman. How I would love to be that selfless, that caring. Help me learn to live for others— as Mary did. And help me to remember, too, that I won't always see the good that comes from what I do. Help me do it just because I love and care—as you did. Teach me how to follow you.

Silent Meditation

Spend a few minutes praying silently about the needs and concerns of family members, coworkers, friends, and your brothers and sisters throughout the world.

Fourteenth Station

Jesus Was Placed in the Tomb

Jesus was placed in a tomb that did not belong to him. Even in death he could claim nothing for his own. Joseph of Arimathea offered this burial place, and Mary must have accepted it with relief and gratitude. Jesus would be buried with dignity.

Personal Reflection

I am a follower of Jesus. I want to believe that God's reward is enough for me. But I find it so hard to let go of my desire for praise and acclaim. I seek all the things that Jesus never sought. How will I ever be the person of faith I so much want to be?

Prayer

Jesus, please help me be more like you. I want to imitate you especially in your role as "tireless teacher." You believed in God's call to preach the good news of the kingdom, and that was enough for you. Help me believe in my call to give witness to you. Help me treasure each person who comes before me as one sent by God. I want to believe. Help my unbelief. Teach me how to follow you.

Silent Meditation

Spend a few minutes praying silently about the needs and concerns of family members, coworkers, friends, and your brothers and sisters throughout the world.

The Resurrection

We are followers of Jesus, called by God to give ourselves to others daily. We "die" daily in many small ways so that others may live more fully. And yet we can claim nothing. We must wait, entombed—in a way—for God's grace to work in us and in those we serve. But Jesus waits with us. He has shown us the way.

We know that Jesus' story did not end on Good Friday. He was raised up by God to new life, and he offers us, too, the promise of resurrection. We, too, are called to be Easter people and Alleluia can be our song—even in the midst of difficult daily occupations.

We have a very important role. Let us continue to daily offer ourselves in loving service to others, until that day when we meet Jesus face to face. No doubt he will embrace us and greet us with these words: "Well done, my good and faithful servant. What you have done for my least ones, you have done for me. Welcome to my kingdom."